STEP OUT,
WALKING ON THE WATER

Sword Ministries International
Branson, Missouri

Walking on Water
Published by:
Sword Ministries International
Branson, MO 65616
ISBN 1-889816-20-5

Introduction

Over the years, I have had many striking visions and dreams of myself in future ministry.

At times, I would see myself preaching to people in large gatherings, even preaching to multitudes in stadiums. Inevitably, the dream would take a turn into the supernatural. Without warning, while ministering to crowds too large to count, I would step out into the miraculous. Shouting words of faith and lifting up the Word of God like a sword, I would see myself walk off a large platform right into the air, a full six feet above the crowd. Then, I would wake up.

For days after, the dream would still resonate in my spirit, calling me to possibilities far beyond my normal, routine existence. The question that came next would always grind on me like a broken record: why should my life be normal and routine? After all, I'd believed as a toddler that Jesus lived inside of me. All my life I knew He gave me life and I knew He was the living Word. Yet, I, like many other Christians, put so many limitations on my life until it became normal and routine. Sure, I would see an occasional healing or miraculous sign. But nothing like what is revealed in the Word. The Word is anything but normal and routine. It is filled with miracles, and no one demonstrated the miraculous more than Jesus did. He fed the five thousand, He raised the dead and He even walked on water.

If Jesus, the living Word, really lived inside me, shouldn't my life reflect the supernatural excitement of the written Word?

The dreams and visions always spurred my faith on. I knew God would not have imprinted them on my spirit so deeply just to tease me with a life that could never be. People are like that. People will lead you on. But not God. He always has a plan to get you there. He always has a plan to build your faith. People tend to complicate things, even people in ministry. But God often uses the simplest things to draw our attention to spiritual truths. He uses basic things in the natural world to teach us because these things are part of His creation. Notice the following verse in Romans:

For since the creation of the world God's invisible qualities, his eternal power and divine nature have been clearly seen, being understood from what has been made, so that men are without excuse.
Romans 1:20 (NIV)

You might not get born again staring at a rock or a lake, but natural things do have God's fingerprints all over them. As Paul makes clear in the above verse, God's power and divine nature are clearly demonstrated in His creation. Lessons of His unlimited power are locked up in natural objects all around us. Jesus made use of this principle more than anyone in His parables. Since He is my example I thought it would be appropriate to use one of these built-in faith lessons.

There is a small lizard native to Tropical America called the Basilisk. This lizard is part of the Iguanid Lizard family native to the Western Hemisphere. The fascinating thing about Basilisk lizards - also called "Jesus Christ lizards"- is their ability to run on their hind legs across the surface of water.

They can actually walk on two legs across small bodies of water.

This lizard does not have webbed feet, as one might suspect. In fact, aside from some small flaps, he has toes similar to that of a human. Yet, he runs right onto the water successfully eluding his enemies. How does he manage? Three things assist him in his feat.

These three things provide us with a great illustration of how we as sons and daughters can step into the supernatural.

Chapter One
Jesus Said Come

Now when evening came, His disciples
went down to the sea, got into the boat,
and went over the sea toward
Capernaum. And it was already dark, and
Jesus had not come to them.
Then the sea arose because a great wind
was blowing.
So when they had rowed about three or
four miles, they saw Jesus walking on the
sea and drawing near the boat; and they
were afraid.
But He said to them, "It is I; do not be
afraid."
Then they willingly received Him into the
boat, and immediately the boat was at the
land where they were going.
John 6:16-21

Immediately the boat was at the land. The miles
instantly vanished. Jesus said the works that I do shall you
do also and greater works, which means when you get into
your car or boat you can immediately take it to where you
are going. All opposition was immediately wiped out when
they received Christ (the Anointed One and His anointing)
walking on the water into the boat. Jesus said "the works
that I do you shall do also and greater works".

It is clear the impossible can be achieved in the
anointing. The boundaries of time and space were

1

eliminated. It is a law of gravity that water cannot hold the natural weight of man. Therefore in order for you to walk on water you must break all natural laws.

Let's take a look at another example in the Word where walking on the water occurred.

Immediately Jesus made His disciples get into the boat and go before Him to the other side, while He sent the multitudes away.
And when He had sent the multitudes away, He went up on the mountain by Himself to pray. Now when evening came, He was alone there.
But the boat was now in the middle of the sea, tossed by the waves, for the wind was contrary.
Now in the fourth watch of the night Jesus went to them, walking on the sea.
And when the disciples saw Him walking on the sea, they were troubled, saying, "It is a ghost!"
And they cried out for fear.
But immediately Jesus spoke to them, saying, "Be of good cheer! It is I; do not be afraid."
And Peter answered Him and said, "Lord, if it is You, command me to come to You on the water."

So He said, "Come." And when Peter had
come down out of the boat, he walked on
the water to go to Jesus.
But when he saw that the wind was
boisterous, he was afraid; and beginning
to sink he cried out, saying, "Lord, save
me!"
And immediately Jesus stretched out His
hand and caught him, and said to him,
"O you of little faith, why did you
doubt?"
And when they got into the boat, the wind
ceased.
Then those who were in the boat came
and worshiped Him, saying, "Truly You
are the Son of God."
When they had crossed over, they came to
the land of Gennesaret.
Matthew 14:22-34

Notice that Peter did not walk on the water until he
had a word from Jesus. He did not say if you can do it then
I can do it. He said 'if it is You Lord then bid me to come',
because if I know I have a Word from You, Lord then I can
do it. But if I don't have a Word from You then I can't do it.
It is the Holy Spirit in Jesus that calls you to do the greater
works. Jesus is speaking by the Spirit. When the Holy
Spirit says come, then you have the go ahead. When the
Holy Spirit says that you can do it, then you can do it.

3

This is How God's Power Works

[1]*"Galatians 5:1 says, "If we live in the Spirit, let us also walk in the Spirit." I believe we should walk in the spirit. I know what it feels like to walk on water. Like Peter, God took me out of the boat a few times. There were times that I felt like I was going to sink. But, what a feeling it is to know that He is there when you're walking on water. I haven't forgotten how to swim. Moving into knowing is a key. Some people are so presumptuous as to think, 'if I do this or that, I'll force Him to move. I'll put away my insulin and I'll force Him to heal this diabetes.' And they die. One man tried to force God by fasting. He said, 'I'll fast until such and such happens.' He died of starvation. Fasting and dying of starvation? Yes, God let him die,*

1 John 2:6 says, "He that saith that he abideth in Him ought himself also to walk as Jesus walked." Walking on water requires hearing the Lord say, "come". If you try to be presumptuous and jump out there in the water thinking, I'll jump out and then God will be required to save me, not so! He might let you drown. Don't get presumptuous with God. Wait till you hear Him speak. Then you can walk on water. 1 John 2:6 American Standard Version says, "Whoever claims to live in Him must walk as Jesus did." To walk as Jesus did! That's our goal. That's what we have to do. We have to learn to walk on water. We must become people of faith..."

---

[1] Walk on Water Or Learn How to Swim, Author Bill Britton, Springfield, Mo

You have to know this is the call of the power of God. In order to hear the call you have to know the Word. The Word has to come to you and you have to come to the realization that you have the Word working on the inside of you in order to believe that you can perform the greater works. If you do not have this knowing inside you then you will not do the impossible.

The call of God is so powerful. Everything in the natural was made from the supernatural and is in subjection to the supernatural call of God. When Jesus said 'come' that one word immediately brought the natural in subjection to the Word of God.

When Peter said, 'Lord, if it is you tell me to come', he waited for the Word of the Lord before stepping out of the boat onto the water. That one Word from God over rode the natural. All of creation is held by the Word, even the angels are subject to the Word of God.

Bless the LORD, you His angels,
Who excel in strength, who do His word,
Heeding the voice of His word.
Psalm 103:20

Therefore all of creation is subject to and bound to obey the command of the Word.

**So He said, "Come." And when Peter had
come down out of the boat, he walked on
the water to go to Jesus.
Matthew 14:29**

All he needed was a Word that would override the natural. Jesus said if you incline your ears unto these sayings and keep them in the midst of your heart and before your eyes they will be health unto your flesh. It does not matter what it looks like or what you are going through. The Word will override and destroy every opposition and cause you to rise above the circumstance.

Peter's step of faith reminds me of this water walking lizard. The most amazing thing about this lizard is that when he is running from his enemies and gets to the water he starts off running while he is still in the water, not while he is on top of the water. He starts in the water and goes to the surface. Some may have to start at the bottom before they reach the top.

Herein lies the connection. At first, Peter relies on the natural law of gravity to float. He is safely on board the boat. Then comes the challenge. Will he trust Jesus and step into the miraculous? Like the lizard, he starts in the natural and goes to the extraordinary. Like Peter, we will not start walking on water until we take that first step from the natural to the supernatural.

You will never know what you are capable of until you step out of the boat.

Chapter Two
Big Feet

The first reason this lizard can walk on water is because he has big feet. How does God see us, what do we look like from His perspective? You have got to realize that as a born again child of God you have "big feet."

I love Psalm 18:26 which says, "You enlarge my steps under me, And my feet have not slipped."

The Bible says that you have been given authority and power to tread upon serpents and scorpions and over all the works of the enemy. Picture it for a moment. This accomplishment takes powerful feet. God wants to give you giant steps. He said that wherever your feet trod, He has given unto you.

"For if you carefully keep all these commandments which I command you to do-- to love the LORD your God, to walk in all His ways, and to hold fast to Him—
"then the LORD will drive out all these nations from before you, and you will dispossess greater and mightier nations than yourselves.
"Every place on which the sole of your foot treads shall be yours: from the wilderness and Lebanon, from the river,

the River Euphrates, even to the Western
Sea, shall be your territory.
"No man shall be able to stand against
you; the LORD your God will put the
dread of you and the fear of you upon all
the land where you tread, just as He has
said to you.
"Behold, I set before you today a blessing
and a curse:
"the blessing, if you obey the
commandments of the LORD your God
which I command you today;
"and the curse, if you do not obey the
commandments of the   LORD your God,
but turn aside from the way which I
command you today, to go after other
gods which you have not known.
Deuteronomy 11:22-28

"Big Feet" means having authority and dominion
every where you walk. A normal man will not be able to
stand against you. When you go to a city, spiritually
speaking you will leave big imprints in it. When you leave
the city, they will know that you came through.

God gave me a vision of going through a city. I saw
myself in the spirit realm with giant feet and I was stepping
over the entire city. I asked the Holy Spirit what was
happening and He said I am giving you dominion over this
city.

God wants to give you giant steps. If you want to move in the supernatural then you need to learn that you have been given authority and power to tread upon serpents and scorpions and over all the works of the enemy. This is what I mean by "big feet."

> **far above all rule and authority and
> power and dominion, and every
> name that is named, not only in this age
> but also in the one to come. And He put
> all things in subjection under His feet,
> and gave Him as head over all things to
> the church, which is His body, the fullness
> of Him who fills all in all.**
> **Eph. 1:21-23**

> **"Behold, I give you the authority
> to trample on serpents and scorpions, and
> over all the power of the enemy, and
> nothing shall by any means hurt you."**
> **Luke 10:19**

> **You are of God, little children, and
> have overcome them, because He who is
> in you is greater than he who is in the
> world.**
> **I John 4:4**

Now step into the revelation that greater is He that is in you than he that is in the world. Your feet have been shod with the preparation of peace. You are not moved by the waves. You are not moved by the circumstances.

9

"But none of these things move me; nor do I count my life dear to myself, so that I may finish my race with joy, and the ministry which I received from the Lord Jesus, to testify to the gospel of the grace of God.
Acts 20:24

What is Paul saying? He is saying none of these things move me. I am overcoming the world. It doesn't matter what is in the world because you are overcoming.

He has "big feet" because in the spirit, his feet represent God-given authority. His feet are bigger than any circumstances that try to say otherwise.

For more information on feet listen to the cd series called *Feet, Feet, Feet.*

Chapter Three
God Weighs All Things in the Balance

The second reason why this lizard can walk on water is because he is light.

He is small and moves quickly and is very skinny. That is a major reason to consider. I was wondering why he needs to be so small and quick. The Holy Spirit said to me, God weighs all things in the balance.

I beseech you therefore brethren by the mercies of God that you present your bodies a living sacrifice holy and acceptable unto God which is your reasonable worship.
Do not be conformed to this world but be transformed by the renewing of your minds that you may prove what is that good and acceptable and perfect will of God.
Romans 12:1-2

In the Old Testament, every time an instrument or utensil was brought into the temple that vessel had to be of an exact precise weight. If the guy who made the golden vessel and utensils brought it to the priest for the temple, and it didn't weigh what it was supposed to weigh, then he had to take it back and remake it to the exact specifications. God has a precise weight for each one of us. There is a spiritual weight that is in perfect harmony with your natural weight. You have to get your natural weight in line with what God has for you. (For more on this subject read my book "The Weightiness of God") This is vitally important for moving in the supernatural.

'You shall do no injustice in judgment, in measurement of length, weight, or volume.
'You shall have honest scales, honest weights, an honest ephah, and an honest hin: I am the LORD your God, who brought you out of the land of Egypt.
Leviticus 19:35-36

Honest weights and scales are the LORD'S; all the weights in the bag are His work.
Proverbs 16:11

Believe it or Not God Needs You

Sin and impurity will act like weights and make you sink to the bottom. You will only have the ability to operate in the supernatural power of God to the degree of the purity of your heart. In purity there will be the power that God desires for you to walk in, spirit, soul and body only this will bring us into the weights that God desires for us.

To operate both in the full expression of God's power that He needs from you, there must be purity. We must be a vessel of honor and glory.

> But in a great house there are not only vessels of gold and silver, but also of wood and clay, some for honor and some for dishonor.
> Therefore if anyone cleanses himself from the latter, he will be a vessel for honor, sanctified and useful for the Master, prepared for every good work.
> Flee also youthful lusts; but pursue righteousness, faith, love, peace with those who call on the Lord out of a pure heart.
> 2 Timothy 2:20-22

God desires to stretch forth His hands through you. In order to do so He needs for you to be of pure spirit, soul and body in order for God to have His full expression in you, through you, and to stretch forth His hand through you. God needs you to touch His people on the earth. You cannot be a tainted vessel, unfit for His use.

> Dishonest scales are an abomination to the LORD, but a just weight is His delight.
> Proverbs 11:1

When pride comes in so does shame, but with humility comes wisdom. God destroyed the children of Israel in the wilderness because they yielded to cravings.

Their physical weight corrupted the spiritual vessel that He had set into place.

Some people have a hard time ministering because they are weak in the flesh, they can only handle so much ministry due to a lack of energy. God is weighing the spirit in the balance both physically, spiritually and in your soul God has a precise weight. This just isn't physical weight it is spiritual weight as well.

You Must Be Light to Walk on Water

Remember the second reason why the lizard is able to walk on water is because he is light.

**"You shall have a perfect and just weight,
a perfect and just measure, that your days
may be lengthened in the land which the
LORD your God is giving you.
Deuteronomy 25:15**

He is talking about physical weight. We see this mirrored in the physical fitness. If you gain too much weight, you shorten your life. Lose weight and you lengthen your life.

That is why this lizard can walk on water. He is light. When we go to certain countries we are only allowed to take a certain amount of luggage due to weight.

We have a weight limit. After all the plane has to be able to leave the earth.

I wonder if God has a weight limit to transportation. God transport me to China. Yeah, and maybe lose five hundred pounds. I am not saying that in a negative way. I am saying that in a positive way. You may have weights of the world dragging behind you. You may have the weight of the love of the world weighing you down.

There are some weights that you have to let go.

Therefore we also, since we are surrounded by so great a cloud of witnesses, let us lay aside every weight, and the sin which so easily ensnares us, and let us run with endurance the race that is set before us,
Hebrews 12:1

This is talking about baggage, the things of the world. God wants to take you through the narrow place.

When you push that camel through the eye of the needle there is no more luggage left on it. You have to squeeze it through, and by the time it gets out of the narrow place, all that is left is the camel and you are squeezing through with it.

"And again I say to you, it is easier for a camel to go through the eye of a needle than for a rich man to enter the kingdom of God."
Matthew 19:24

In order for a camel to go through the eye of a needle you would have to strip him down and squeeze him through. Likewise God is trying to take you somewhere.

An excellent example of this is Abraham and Lot. God said 'Abraham, go to the Promised Land.' but He *didn't say* to take Lot.

God said Abraham 'I want to take you to a new place' and who comes along, old nephew Lot. Lot represents the voice from the past familiar with his uncle. This voice from the past wants to manipulate its way into your future.

It is called Lot. Lot was weight.

Where God wants to take you Lot cannot go. If you take him with you, you are going to end up with Sodom and Gomorrah. You are going to end up fighting for Lot's life. The biggest weight Abraham had was Lot. Lot was an anchor holding Abraham down.

Sometimes weight can be something hanging around you keeping you from being what God wants you to be. You will end up dividing your cattle with him, you will end up with a war on your hands because you stopped on the way to where you were going; somewhere that God didn't tell somebody else to go. These voices from the past can become weights on you dragging you down, holding you back and keeping you from *walking on the water.*

**Then the LORD rained brimstone and
fire on Sodom and Gomorrah, from the
LORD out of the heavens.
So He overthrew those cities, all the plain,
all the inhabitants of the cities, and what
grew on the ground.
But his wife looked back behind him, and
she became a pillar of salt.
Genesis 19:24-26**

When we allow ourselves to stay in the past we will become like Lot's wife a pillar of salt worth less than nothing because we have allowed the past to hold us back.

**But Jesus said to him, "No one, having
put his hand to the plow, and looking
back, is fit for the kingdom of God."
Luke 9:62**

Old things are past away. Forget it, it is gone and over. There is no way you can go back and change the past. It is over. It doesn't help us move forward to go back and try to fix the past.

**Brethren, I do not count myself to have
apprehended; but one thing I do,
forgetting those things which are behind
and reaching forward to those things
which are ahead,
I press toward the goal for the prize of the
upward call of God in Christ Jesus.
Philippians 3:13-14**

One of the greatest things that you can do is forget those things, which are behind. Eliminate the weights. You have to be light if you want to go places with God that you have never gone before. We won't be light if we are carrying around the weights and cares of the world.

**"Come to Me, all you who labor and are
heavy laden, and I will give you rest.
"Take My yoke upon you and learn from
Me, for I am gentle and lowly in heart,
and you will find rest for your souls.
"For My yoke is easy and My burden is
light."
Matthew 11:28-30**

Weight and the Eagle

There is an eagle in Australia that gets a tumor on his beak. When he gets the tumor on his beak, the way that he gets rid of it is to fly as high as he can and go to an atmospheric level that no other creature or bird can go.

When he gets to that height, he does everything that he can to lift himself even higher. He then takes himself to the place where his body feels like it is about to explode because of the atmospheric pressure. When he does this he senses the atmospheric pressure until he feels like his body is about to burst. When he knows he is at this point he forces his beak into this atmospheric pressure and at that point the tumor on his beak bursts off. Suddenly, he falls down totally healed of the tumor that was on him.

He broke free of the weight that was keeping him from walking on the water. He broke free of the weights of the world that were holding him down. Some of you need to take your mouth into the presence of God and leave it there until the cancer is gone and broken off. Some people have a weight on their mouth; they need to take their mouth into the presence of God. When they get their mouth into the presence of God they will speak what God wants them to speak and nothing else.

Even so the tongue is a little member and boasts great things. See how great a forest a little fire kindles!
And the tongue is a fire, a world of iniquity. The tongue is so set among our members that it defiles the whole body, and sets on fire the course of nature; and it is set on fire by hell.
For every kind of beast and bird, of reptile and creature of the sea, is tamed and has been tamed by mankind.

But no man can tame the tongue. It is an
unruly evil, full of deadly poison.
with it we bless our God and Father, and
with it we curse men, who have been
made in the similitude of God.
Out of the same mouth proceed blessing
and cursing. My brethren, these things
ought not to be so.
Does a spring send forth fresh water and
bitter from the same opening?
Can a fig tree, my brethren, bear
olives, or a grapevine bear figs
Thus no spring can yield both salt water
and fresh.
James 3:5-12

But those who wait on the LORD shall
renew their strength; they shall mount up
with wings like eagles, they shall run and
not be weary, they shall walk and not
faint.
Isaiah 40:31

Chapter Four
Walking On the Water Requires Obedience

The third reason the lizard can walk on water has to do with speed.

The Lizard is Fast

I believe that carries great implication. The quicker that you obey God the quicker He is going to move because the power of God is released to the degree that obedience is exercised and no more. The quicker that you obey God, the quicker that you will go where God wants you to go.

Some people run into brick walls all their lives. They go through so much; it is because when God told them to do something they didn't move fast with God.

You have to obey quickly. When He says come on the water, get out of the boat and don't think, just do it.

I believe there are people on this earth today who desire to walk the way Jesus walked.

**If we live in the Spirit, let us also walk in
the Spirit.
Galatians 5:25**

He who says he abides in Him ought
himself also to walk
just as He walked.
I John 2:6

Jesus brings us faith to obey and to move quickly in the realm of the Spirit.

In order to walk on water we must be able to hear with clarity the voice of the Lord.

When He tells us to come out to Him on the water we must have hearing ears to hear what the Spirit is saying. We must wait until we hear His voice and not just walk out in presumption. The New American Standard says, "Whoever claims to live in Him must walk as Jesus did".

In order to do this we must walk in faith. Faith comes by hearing, and hearing by the word of God.

So then faith comes by hearing, and
hearing by the word of God.
Romans 10:17

Walking on Water Is a Step of Faith

Walking on water takes practice, the practice of faith. One cannot just simply walk on the water at random without first believing that he can do so. Walking on the

22

water means taking a step of faith out on water that is possibly stormy. But if we wait and take that step when we hear the voice of the Master call us to 'come' then we are stepping out at His Word and His Word never returns void. It always produces. It always accomplishes that which it has been sent forth to accomplish.

When Jesus called Peter to come, Peter did not hesitate he just started walking. He obeyed the voice of the Master in faith and stepped out into the storm. Now he did sink but that is only because he began looking at the situation around him. The stormy seas represent the situation and circumstances we all face. When we walk on water we must keep a right spirit and we must keep our vision focused on the Master of the water, then we will walk on top.

Remember the Holy Spirit is in Jesus calling you to do the greater works.

For we walk by faith, not by sight.
2 Corinthians 5:7

When we were in Pittsburg, Kansas before the first service even began, a lady died in the lobby of the auditorium where we were having services. My staff and I walked into the area where she was laying dead and the first thing that happened was my mind attempting to take over.

Everyone was standing around in fear, saying she is dead, it is over. I moved quickly and said, "Stop the fear!" and we began to pray.

We rebuked death and commanded resurrection power, the power of God, to hit that lady and she was raised from the dead!

I believe the reason she was raised from the dead was because we didn't allow our minds the opportunity to meditate on death. I moved quickly.

You don't have to wait for God to tell you to raise someone from the dead. We don't have time for that.

The Word says, "these signs shall follow them that believe; you shall cast out devils, heal the sick and raise the dead."

He told you to raise the dead. It is a *command*.

"Heal the sick, cleanse the lepers, raise the dead, cast out demons. Freely you have received, freely give.
Matthew 10:8

Remember walking by faith and not by sight does not mean blind faith.

"I will lead the blind by a way they do not know, In paths they do not know I will guide them. I will make darkness into light before them And rugged places into plains. These are the things I will do, And I will not leave them undone."
Isaiah 42:16

Present truth produces now faith. Revelation acted upon can lift you above various circumstances. The Word is a lamp unto your feet.

Step Out today!

Chapter Five
Stepping Out In Power

God is looking for those that have disciplined themselves for quick obedience. We want to get power. God is saying I want discipline. You need to learn how to get big feet and to know who you are in Christ Jesus.

Learn to get the weight that He desires for you.

Learn to obey God quickly if you want power.

That lizard is pretty amazing. He is able to walk on water because of:

- *big feet,*
- *he moves fast*
- *he's light*

I for one have missed God, sometimes in such a big way, in the Spirit.

Once while I was in Fremont, Nebraska God told me to walk off the stage. I saw angels in the meetings ministering to people. There were a lot of supernatural things happening in that meeting. I closed my eyes and walked to the edge of the stage and God said "just walk in the air above the people's heads and everywhere you walk they are going to have a miracle". It was a high stage.

I walked to the end of the stage and looked down and said "are you sure about this Holy Spirit"? My mind kicked in and I thought "no, this is the end of the stage, gravity". My mind kicked in and was saying it is impossible, but if I had obeyed quickly it would not have been impossible.

That night I had a vision and God showed me in the vision every thing that would have happened if I had obeyed Him instantly.

The key here is to *obey quickly*.

When people do not accept divine guidance, they run wild. But whoever obeys the law is happy.
Proverbs 29:18 (NLT)

Where there is no vision, the people perish: but he that keepeth the law, happy is he.
Proverbs 29:18 (KJV)

As we walk as Jesus walked it is important for us to walk where our vision is. We can't settle for where we are now, because if we do we are settling for less.

God gave Abraham a vision for a son and for the land that he would possess. When Sarah died Abraham had to buy the land he was dwelling in just to bury her. God had given Abraham a vision to possess the land wherein he dwelt, but at the time of Sarah's death he still had yet to possess the land.   Abraham had yet to walk fully in the place of his vision.

Sarah lived one hundred and twenty-
seven years; these were the years of the
life of Sarah.
Then Abraham stood up from before his
dead, and spoke to the sons of Heth,
saying,
"I am a foreigner and a sojourner among
you. Give me property for a burial place
among you, that I may bury my dead out
of my sight."
Then Abraham stood up and bowed
himself to the people of the land, the sons
of Heth.
And he spoke with them, saying, "If it is
your wish that I bury my dead out of my
sight, hear me, and meet with Ephron the
son of Zohar for me,
"that he may give me the cave of
Machpelah which he has, which is at the
end of his field. Let him give it to me at
the full price, as property for a burial
place among you."
"No, my lord, hear me: I give you the
field and the cave that is in it; I give it to
you in the presence of the sons of my
people. I give it to you. Bury your dead!"
Then Abraham bowed himself down
before the people of the land;

and he spoke to Ephron in the hearing of
the people of the land, saying, "If you will
give it, please hear me. I will give you
money for the field; take it from me and I
will bury my dead there."
So the field of Ephron which was in
Machpelah, which was before Mamre, the
field and the cave which was in it, and all
the trees that were in the field, which
were within all the surrounding borders,
were deeded
to Abraham as a possession in the
presence of the sons of Heth, before all
who went in at the gate of his city.
And after this, Abraham buried Sarah his
wife in the cave of the field of Machpelah,
before Mamre (that is, Hebron) in the
land of Canaan.
Genesis 23:1,3-4,7-9,11-13,17-19

Later when Joshua came along with the children of
Israel God told him that every where they walked they
would possess the land. This promise came about because
of their original fear upon entering the land. They saw the
giants and had instant fear that they were unable to possess
all of the land that they tread upon.

They were unable to possess the land belonging to
Esau and to Lot.

When we walk in the supernatural it is important that we:

1. Walk with God.

And Enoch walked with God; and he was not, for God took him.
Genesis 5:24

2. Walk after God.

You shall walk after the LORD your God and fear Him, and keep His commandments and obey His voice; you shall serve Him and hold fast to Him
Deuteronomy 13:4

3. Walk before God.

When Abram was ninety-nine years old, the LORD appeared to Abram and said to him, "I am Almighty God; walk before Me and be blameless
Genesis 17:1

4. Walk in God.

As you therefore have received Christ Jesus the Lord, so walk in Him,
Colossians 2:6

To walk on the water you must keep your eyes on Jesus, the Author and Finisher of our Faith. You must leave the familiar behind to experience the unfamiliar which is ahead in the power of God.

I believe these four keys will help you be a water-walking disciple.

The children of Israel walked in the place of Abraham's vision. Abraham did not settle for where he was walking, he continued to believe so that when Joshua and the children of Israel came along, they just picked up the walk where Abraham left off.

Basically they carried on Abraham's vision for him. They possessed the land and the vision that God had given to Abraham so many years before.

**He did not waver at the promise of God through unbelief, but was strengthened in faith, giving glory to God, and being fully convinced that what He had promised He was also able to perform.
And therefore "it was accounted to him for righteousness."
Romans 4:20-22**

I have had many visions of seeing myself go places and working all kinds of signs and wonders. But many times instead of stepping out in myself to accomplish what

God has shown me I wait for God's timing to end up in the place of the vision.

This happened to me once in Tennessee. I knew that there were four people in that place who were going to have miracles. That morning when I walked into the crusade that place was already in my vision and I knew four miracles were going to take place. The minute I walked in, the vision came alive. I had seen that church in a vision five years before.

I walked up to this man and said, "I know exactly what is wrong with you," and the power of God answered miraculously. I walked up to a lady and said, "I see your leg grow right now." She hit the aisle and sure enough, her leg grew about five inches.

When I walked into that church everything that I had done in my dream came into manifestation down to the last detail.

I could have stood there and just thought about it and said well maybe the dream was just a *pizza dream.*

God isn't going to give you a supernatural *pizza dream.* God isn't going to give you a dream of arms and legs growing by *pizza.* He will do it by Himself.

He Will Do It from His Spirit

**"And it shall come to pass afterward that
I will pour out My Spirit on all flesh; your
sons and your daughters shall prophesy,
your old men shall dream dreams, your
young men shall see visions.**

Joel 2:28

God wants to give you creative visions and dreams.

During the past several years, I have had many visions and dreams of walking in the air. One night I saw myself walking in the air over buildings. Once during one of these visions I noticed that when I got entangled in people's emotions I would be drawn back to the earth. In the spirit, I would look not for the steps but I would feel for the steps. It literally felt like God was holding each step up. As I walked in the air relating with the Lord we were on a continual flow as if He was walking with me and through me and in me. It was as if we walked together as one.

**And Enoch walked with God; and he was
not, for God took him.
Genesis 5:24**

In another dream, I walked in a stadium filled with businessmen. As we walked through the air, the Lord had me take the mike from the leading speaker. As I did, I began to declare God's supernatural power and salvation to all. During this entire time, I was eight feet above the ground walking over the people's head's while I preached!

This may sound strange to people but God desires to set into place dreams of patterns in your consciousness to prepare you for a great supernatural work.

The following is an excerpt from Franklin Hall's book "The Return of Immortality".

[2]*"There was a humble saint living by the name of Brother Martin de Porres. He had the Holy Spirit so strongly upon his body that he felt that he had no legs at all. In fact, may times he felt weightless and lifted up. Sometimes he actually ascended up into space. The Lord actually raised him up. Brother Martin was therefore given a nickname: "Flying Brother". Brother Martin had very accurate prophetical foresight about things.*

The Flying Space-Flight Brother

The Flying Brother was found in different countries at times, far away from his native country, Lima, Peru, where he was born in 1579. He astounded many folk by doing the extraordinary. He prophesied the future as a prophet of God. What he prophesied came about as he declared it. He also could get the sick healed by the prayer of faith, Jesus' dear name. There were many witnesses to

---

[2]Taken from the book The Return of Immortality by Franklin Hall copyright 1976 by Hall Deliverance FDN. Inc. taken from the introduction, also pages 22 and 23

his many miracles and he was the talk of the subject of some author's books at that time. Brother Martin had many amazing supernatural Holy Ghost Experiences.

Brother Martin Had Immortality Experiences

Many of his colleagues, as well as the entire Spanish colony of Peru, were astounded by his supernatural miracles, and were witnesses to the facts of the same. A number witnessed that they saw the Flying Brother raised up from the ground and the forces of gravitation, hovering motionless almost four feet from the ground.

At another time a number saw him raised up high above the earth in a floating, motionless position for some time. Others have seen the Flying Brother take a space, translation flight without gravitation limitations, at great distances. After all, why should this seem unusual when Brother Phillip, of the early church took a space flight. Also, the Sun Clothed Woman will take space translation flights and her manchild will have translation to God's throne and back.

As more and more Immortality is put upon our bodies; Jesus said, "I will raise him up". When? In the last days. How? As one gets on the menu that endures everlasting life. A menu of Immortality FOOD from the Now Jesus Body (John 6).

The Flying Brother made instantaneous, translation flights to a number of countries where he was reported, authentically seen and seen by those who knew him

36

personally. Some of these space flight trips were to bless certain saints in Mexico, in the Philippines, in China, Japan and in other places. Some of those blessed, were in institutions and in great despair.

An authoress, Doris Burton wrote about his miracles. another author who had witnessed his miracles personally, Don Mervelo Rivera, also wrote about his miracles and mentioned the names, affidavits of several priests and prophets who likewise witnessed them.

A Spanish brother, Francisco de Vega Montoga, verifies seeing them. The Flying Brother could fly right through locked doors. Even stonewalls were no barrier for him to get through. No locked jail or building was an obstacle to him. Paul and Silas, also Peter, along with other Bible characters, who were imprisoned, had the locked chains fall from their bodies and locked prison doors to come open. Brother Martin could enter hospitals and prisons and help those who were discouraged and sick. Many were delivered. Through Jesus Christ, he would get many sick folk healed that the doctors could not cure."

You have to meditate upon the supernatural if you want to experience it.

You have to meditate on His creation, on all His signs and wonders. Meditate upon Him dividing the Red Sea, causing the sun to stand still, pouring manna down from heaven.

He performed all those miracles through men.

You have been given "big feet," spiritually speaking. He has given you dominion. You are commanded to go out and possess the land. This is one of the greatest tools that Islam uses against Christianity. They say, 'our God gives us land,' and they take it for their god Allah.

"Every place on which the sole of your
foot treads shall be yours: from the
wilderness and Lebanon, from the river,
the River Euphrates, even to the Western
Sea, shall be your territory.
"No man shall be able to stand against
you; the LORD your God will put the
dread of you and the fear of you upon all
the land where you tread, just as He has
said to you.
"Behold, I set before you today a blessing
and a curse:
"the blessing, if you obey the
commandments of the LORD your God
which I command you today;
Deuteronomy 11:24-27

God wants to give everyone visions and dreams. God promises these to all of His children. Some people are simply more prepared for them than others.

I was thinking about the parable of the bridegroom and the ten virgins. Five of them had their lamps full of oil and five didn't.   Instead of preparing they allowed themselves to be distracted by the weights of the world.

"Then the kingdom of heaven shall be likened to ten virgins who took their lamps and went out to meet the bridegroom.
"Now five of them were wise, and five were foolish.
"Those who were foolish took their lamps and took no oil with them,
Matthew 25:1-4

A Final Thought

God is admonishing us to be the son and daughter of God that we are called to be.

He is saying "Get ready". He wants to pour out His Spirit in new and fresh ways. If we aren't ready when the Spirit gets poured out in a fresh new way different than we are used to then we question it.

Have we been taking time to get to know God more than we did yesterday? I have been a Christian since Pentecost first started. I know it all. You don't need to tell me anything.

It is the same Spirit, but it might be a different manifestation.

There are diversities of gifts, but the same
Spirit.
There are differences of ministries, but
the same Lord.
And there are diversities of activities, but
it is the same God who works all in all.
But the manifestation of the Spirit is
given to each one for the profit of all:
1 Corinthians 12: 4-7

That is why the Bible tells us to renew our minds, to get into God's presence daily. So that we are able to recognize when He does something just a little bit different

41

than what we have seen before. We won't criticize and miss out.

God Doesn't Want You to Miss Out!!

I urge you therefore, brethren, by the mercies of God, to present your bodies a living and holy sacrifice, acceptable to God, {which is} your spiritual service of worship.
And do not be conformed to this world, but be transformed by the renewing of your mind, that you may prove what the will of God is, that which is good and acceptable and perfect.
Romans 12:1-2 (NAS)

Mark 4:2-3 talks about the sower sowing the Word. He who has ears to hear let Him hear what God says. You have to have a hearing ear and understand what God says.

As we look in the mirror beholding the Lord we are changed from glory to glory. Some people like to stand before the mirror and behold themselves. We need to stand before the mirror and behold God in the same manner that we behold ourselves. We need to get that way with God and His presence. God wants us to be so intimate with him that we see Him when we look into the mirror.

**But we all, with unveiled face, beholding
as in a mirror the glory of the Lord, are
being transformed into the same image
from glory to glory, just as by the Spirit of
the Lord.
2 Corinthians 3:18**

Firstly, in a practical sense when it comes to the Christian life, when it is time to walk on the water it must be decided upon and obeyed. When we obey God and step out of the boat the first thought we have may be initial shock or the feeling that we are doing something we have never done before.

At this point don't allow any mental blocks of doubt, fear, or insecurity to enter and take control in your mind!

Once you step into this spiritual realm in faith, living this supernatural freedom is as natural as breathing. Limitations are broken.

Second, don't analyze and criticize why Peter started sinking! You don't need faith in the boat. Remember faith without works is dead. Focus on Jesus, the Author and Finisher of our Faith and step out and do the Great Commission.

Third, to walk on the water you must step out to where He is, in passionate hunger beyond human reason, totally committing yourself to the life of faith in His presence.

Another reason why people are apathetic towards God is they have not fully committed to the higher life Jesus is calling them to. Many have become comfortable at doing things their own way.

God ahead step into God's way! Watch the adrenaline of the Holy Spirit rise enabling you to reach for the high calling of God in Christ Jesus.

Trust His promises.

Peter may have begun to sink but he did something others only dream of.

Dr. Oral Roberts always used to say:
"When you see the invisible, you will do the impossible!"

God ahead and step out and walk on water. Don't be afraid to step out of the boat. Don't hesitate to obey God. Use your authority. Stay quick and light.

Then you won't miss out on the greatest blessings you can imagine.

About the Author

Warren Hunter is the Founder and President of Sword Ministries International. Born in South Africa, he was raised under the influence of many well known ministers. At the age of thirteen, he began a ministry leading weekly Bible studies for his fellow students. After arriving in America, he received seven years of higher education in Tulsa, Oklahoma, which included Oral Roberts University.

In 1988 Sword Ministries International was launched as a Non-Profit Organization. Through ministering on the streets, traveling weekends, writing books, and much prayer, Warren's ministry has expanded within the call of God on his life.

To date Warren has authored more than twenty five books and teaching manuals and has dozens of teaching series as well as hundreds of individual audio teachings. As a young boy in South Africa, he assisted his grandfather Bernard Hunter in building many churches. Warren has seen thousands come to Christ not only in South Africa, but worldwide through this ministry and especially in Central Africa over the last decade.

Today, He lives in Branson, Missouri with his wife and six children. Warren is an internationally known speaker who conducts hundreds of meetings every year in addition to a daily live streamed bible study. His vision is to touch the world with a vibrant and unlimited move of God, effecting lasting changes in hearts and lives with signs and wonders following decently and in order by the power of the Holy Spirit.

Apostolic Sword Network

As you read through the ASN Manual, you will begin to see Apostolic Revivalist Warren Hunter's heart for kingdom connections and pure covenant father-son relationships.

As a member of ASN you are a member of the Sword Ministries International family and are a part of the big picture as we touch the world through a vibrant move of the power and demonstration of God's Spirit through signs, wonders and miracles.

Within the manual you will also find information about being licensed and/or ordained through the Apostolic Sword Network. Please visit the Five Pillar Visionary Structure to see the *bigness* of the vision that God has for Sword Ministries International and how you can be a part of it!

Once you have read and prayed through the manual, you may contact us and we will answer any other questions you may have.

Find the *Apostolic Sword Network Manual* for free online at: www.swordministries.org/apostolic-sword-network

Sword Ministries Resource Library

Books

- 35 Reasons Healing is God's Will
- Divine Attraction
- From Fire to Glory
- God Working With God
- Growing in Confidence
- How to Birth a Miracle
- Is Your Perception a Weapon
- Keys to a Yielded Will
- Presenting a Yielded Will
- Supply of the Spirit
- The Breath of the Almighty
- The Glory of the Anointing
- The Lightenings of God
- The Power of a Consecrated Heart
- The Power of Innocence
- The Vision of the Seed
- The Weightiness of God
- Think Like God
- Touch Not my Anointed
- Transparency
- Unlimited Realm Vol. 1
- Unlimited Realm Vol. 2
- Visionaries: Rise to Leadership
- Visionaries: Set Your Sights Higher
- Walking on Water

Audio Series

- Awakening Prophetic Purpose
- Divine Attraction
- Faith 101
- Faith for Life
- First Fruits
- Force of a Recreated Spirit
- God Hears Himself
- God Working With God Vol 1
- Grace for Life
- Holy Spirit in the Old Covenant
- I Am Who I Am
- Jesus Like Leadership
- Kingdom Power
- Living in the Cloud
- Love Defined
- Nature of Miracles
- New Wine
- Raising Warriors in a Cave
- The Fragrance of Christ
- The Secret of God
- Tuning in to the Voice of God
- Uncapping the Forces of God Within
- Who are You? ID in Christ

Training Manuals + DVD

- Called to Call
- Concerning Spirituals
- Flowing in the Supernatural
- Focus
- Increase the Anointing

- Leading with Power through Apostolic Thrust
- The Prophetic Spirit
- Supernatural Leadership Training Institute
- Wisdom for Signs and Wonders

These and much more available through the Sword Ministries web store: **www.swordministries.org**

Sword Ministries International

For information or further resources please contact Sword Ministries through the following channels.

Write to:

Sword Ministries International
P.O. Box 7360
Branson, MO 65616

Email:
info@swordministries.org

Website:
www.swordministries.org

US Ministry Office:
(417) 544 - 0838

Social Media:
Find us on **Facebook, Youtube, LinkedIn**, etc

www.ingramcontent.com/pod-product-compliance
Lightning Source LLC
Chambersburg PA
CBHW071733020426
42331CB00008B/2018